AF316705

WHY IS DADDY ALWAYS MAD?

NATASHA FRAZIER, LCSW

www.1000storybooks.com

DEDICATION

I want to thank my mother, Maria, who is my first fan and exemplifies sacrificial love. She taught me the definition of service and to help others, regardless of the size of the contribution. Secondly, I want to thank my husband, Aaron, who has encouraged me to think big and not be afraid to live out my dreams. Lastly, I want to thank my family and closest friends who have provided encouragement, support and have always stood by my side.

"Do you think Dad loves us, Sophia?" said Adam as he bashed his action heroes together.

Sophia looked up from her book. "Why would you say something like that?"

"Doesn't it bother you when he slams the door and yells? And when he just sits in front of the TV when he comes home from work." Adam furrowed his eyebrows and scrunched his nose up, mimicking the face their dad always made. "And he never plays with us."

"Well, he loves us. He just doesn't like to play. That's not a big deal," said Sophia, shrugging her shoulders.

As Adam turned his attention again to his action heroes, he heard his dad begin to raise his voice in the kitchen. The siblings looked at each other at the same time and Sophia stood up and closed the bedroom door.

"Shhh, the kids can hear you, Mark. Lower your voice," whispered Mom from the kitchen.

CLICK!!

As Dad's voice lowered, Mom called, "Kids, dinner. Time to come downstairs."

Adam and Sophia ran into the kitchen, sliding into their seats.

"Did you wash your hands?" Dad said with a scowl.

Adam and Sophia moved slowly to the kitchen sink.

"Why must I always remind you guys to wash your hands?" Dad said, voice raising. "Don't you know by now that you have to wash your hands before coming to the table? You're not babies."

"Stop that, Mark. Don't start in front of the children," said Mom. Dad ignored her and took a sip of his beverage.

Adam returned to the kitchen table, avoiding eye contact as Sophia slid into her seat next to him.

Mom put her hands on her hips and glared at Dad, encouraging him to reassure the children.

"I'm sorry, kids," Dad said. "I didn't mean to yell at you. I just want you to remember basics like washing your hands before mealtime."

"Yes, Dad," chimed Sophia and Adam at the same time, keeping their gaze at the plate in front of them.

The next morning, Adam walked into the kitchen to find his Dad making breakfast. "Hey kiddo," Dad said. "Do you want waffles for breakfast?"

"Uh, sure," said Adam, stopping in his tracks when he realized he was alone.

He quietly sat down at the table, hoping that his mother or sister would come join him.

Dad placed the plate of waffles and eggs in front of Adam.

"Thank you," mumbled Adam, keeping his gaze on the plate.

"How is school, son?" asked Dad as he went back to making more waffles.

"It's good." Adam pushed the eggs around his plate.

During recess the next day, Adam was playing kickball. "No, stupid you don't play that way," yelled Adam. He pushed his classmate, Liam, to the ground.

Liam started crying. Adam's teacher ran to Liam, putting her arms around him.

After helping Liam to his feet, Adam's teacher turned her attention to Adam. "Adam, what you said and did to Liam was wrong. We do not call people mean names or push them. I'm going to have to tell your parents about what just happened here."

Adam whimpered as he walked back into the school, his shoulders slumped.

When Mom picked Adam and Sophia up later that day, the teacher asked to speak to Mom.

"Uh oh, what did you do this time, Adam?" Sophia asked.

"I didn't do anything. I just pushed Liam during recess. He was being stupid and not playing by the rules."

"Why?" asked Sophia as Mom returned, her lips pursed.

"Adam, I am not happy about the report I just received from Ms. Rachel. Why would you call Liam a bad name and push him? Daddy and I have taught you better than that."

Adam started to cry.

DANCE
DAY

"You know I'm going to have to tell Dad," Mom said.

"Please don't tell him," Adam whispered. "He's only going to yell at me more."

Mom turned around in the driver's seat, shocked. "Why would you say that?"

"Because Dad doesn't love me."

Mom's face softened as she touched Adam's knee. "Oh, no, sweetheart, Daddy loves you. Dad just—Daddy just works very hard and has a lot on his mind, but it has nothing to do with you and Sophia."

Sophia reached over to hold her brother's hand, giving him a half-hearted smile.

Adam and Sophia were doing their homework in the dining room when Dad got home.

"Hi, kids. How was school today?"

"It was good," Sophia said quickly. She looked at her brother and gulped.

"Adam, how was your day?" asked Dad.

"It was okay," Adam said, barely above a whisper.

At that moment, Mom entered the room, "Mark, can you come into the kitchen with me as I prepare dinner? I need to speak with you."

As Dad left the room, Sophia stroked Adam's arm.

"Son, come here," said Dad.

Adam stood up and walked toward the kitchen with his head down.

"Mom told me about what happened today."

Adam kept his eyes on the floor.

"I'm very disappointed about what happened with Liam. I thought he was your friend. But I'm sad about what you said to Mom in the car. Why would you say that?"

"I... I didn't mean that, Dad. I don't know why I said it," Adam said.

"Can you please look at me, Adam? You don't have to be afraid of me."

Adam slowly glanced up to meet his eyes.

"It's okay, you can be honest. I won't get upset," Dad said.

"Well...sometimes I can hear you yelling and slamming doors. It scares me."

Dad looked at Adam with tears in his eyes and sighed. "I'm sorry that my yelling scares you. I promise you that I'm not mad at you when I yell. Do you think you can give me another chance?" Adam smiled at his Dad. He nodded.

Dad pulled Adam in for a hug. "You and Sophia make me so happy. It's just that sometimes Daddy doesn't know how to use his words when he gets upset."

"But I promise I'm going to start trying. I don't want you to ever think I don't love you."

Dad tucked Adam in bed for the night. "You know, son, I love you very much. I don't want you to ever be afraid of me. When I was your age, I used to be scared of Grandpa. He would yell a lot and I would go into the bedroom that I shared with Uncle Kevin, and we would huddle together until he stopped."

Adam looked at his dad as Dad leaned in to kiss him on the forehead.

Dad closed the door to Adam's bedroom and walked quietly to the kitchen as Mom made the children's school lunches for tomorrow.

Dad sat at the table as Mom joined him.

He pulled a card out of his wallet and dialed a number. "Hi, is this Angela?"

He waited for her reply as he looked nervously at Mom.

"Hi, yes, I—um—my kids are afraid of me. I think I have anger issues and I'd like to set up a meeting to talk with you."

Dad listened and nodded.

"Yes, next Tuesday at 6 p.m. works for me."

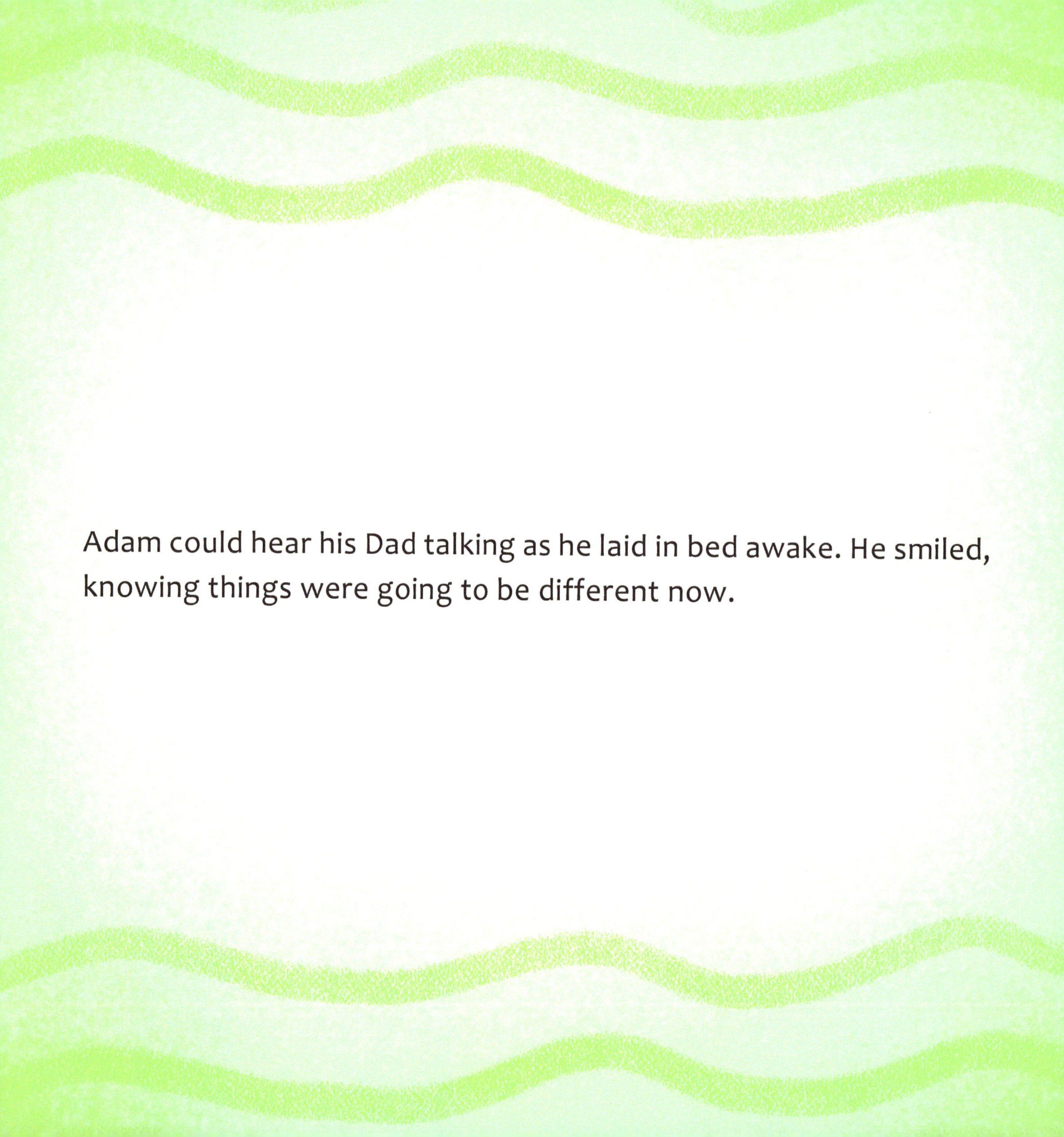

Adam could hear his Dad talking as he laid in bed awake. He smiled, knowing things were going to be different now.

"Dad, quick I have all of our superheroes lined up," said Adam eagerly.

"Coming, son," said Dad as he walked over to Adam.

The End.

If you or someone you know would like to speak to an individual about issues such as anger, please contact your:

School Counselor
Employee Assistance Program (through employer)
Health Insurance (to identify an in-network provider)

Natasha Frazier has been a social worker for over 15 years working with children, families, and the geriatric population. Her love for children started young, assisting her mother as a Sunday School volunteer and eventually working with elementary school children as a tutor and in community organizations.